Miley Cyrus
Rock Star

Maggie Murphy

PowerKids press.

New York

Published in 2011 by The Rosen Publishing Group, Inc.
29 East 21st Street, New York, NY 10010

First Edition

Book Design: Greg Tucker
Photo Researcher: Jessica Gerweck

Photo Credits: Cover, pp. 8–9, 10–11, 12–13 Kevin Mazur/
Wirelmage/Getty Images; pp. 4–5 Charley Gallay/Getty Images; p. 7
Joerg Koch/AFP/Getty Images; p. 15 Miguel Villagran/Getty Images;
p. 17 Eric Charbonneau/Le Studio/Wirelmage/Getty Images; p. 19
Kevin Winter/Getty Images; pp. 20–21 Frank Micelotta/Getty Images
for MTV; p. 22 Steve Granitz/Wirelmage.

Library of Congress Cataloging-in-Publication Data

Murphy, Maggie.
  Miley Cyrus : rock star / Maggie Murphy. — 1st ed.
     p. cm. — (Young and famous)
  Includes index.
  ISBN 978-1-4488-0643-0 (library binding) —
ISBN 978-1-4488-1799-3 (pbk.) — ISBN 978-1-4488-1800-6 (6-pack)
  1. Cyrus, Miley, 1992—Juvenile literature. 2. Singers—United States—
Biography—Juvenile literature. 3. Television actors and actresses—United
States—Biography—Juvenile literature. 4. Motion picture actors and
actresses—United States—Biography—Juvenile literature. I. Title.
  ML3930.C98M87 2011
  782.42164092—dc22
  [B]
                    2009046868

Manufactured in the United States of America

CPSIA Compliance Information: Batch #WS10PK: For Further Information contact Rosen Publishing, New York, New York at
1-800-237-9932

Contents

Miley Cyrus is a rock star. She was born in Nashville, Tennessee, in 1992.

Miley is also an actress. She has acted on TV shows and in movies.

She stars in *Hannah Montana*. This TV show made her **famous**.

Miley loves to write songs. She sings and plays guitar and piano.

Miley often goes on tour. This means she plays **concerts** all over the world.

Miley's father is a country music singer. His name is Billy Ray Cyrus.

Some of Miley's friends are also famous. Taylor Swift is her good friend.

Miley has won many **awards**. She won a 2009 MTV Movie Award.

Miley's fans think she has a lot of **talent**. She loves to meet her fans.

Miley hopes to keep making music for a long time.

Books

Here are more books to read about Miley Cyrus:

Berne, Emma Carlson. *Miley Cyrus.* New York: Scholastic Library Publishing, 2009.

Franks, Katie. *Miley Cyrus.* Kid Stars! New York: PowerKids Press, 2009.

Web Sites

Due to the changing nature of Internet links, PowerKids Press has developed an online list of Web sites related to the subject of this book. This site is updated regularly. Please use this link to access the list:
www.powerkidslinks.com/young/mc/

Glossary

awards (uh-WORDZ) Honors given to people.

concerts (KONT-serts) Public musical performances.

famous (FAY-mus) Very well known.

talent (TA-lent) A natural ability or skill.

Index